See how plants grow

Vegetables

Nicola Edwards

WAYLAND

Copyright © Wayland 2006
Editor: Penny Worms
Senior Design Manager: Rosamund Saunders
Designer: Elaine Wilkinson

Published in Great Britain in 2006 by Wayland,
an imprint of Hachette Children's Books

British Library Cataloguing in Publication Data
Edwards, Nicola
    Vegetables. - (See how they grow)
    1. Vegetables - Juvenile literature
    I. Title
    635

ISBN 10: 0 7502 4907 2
ISBN 13: 978 0 7502 4907 2

Printed in China
Wayland
An imprint of Hachette Children's Books
338 Euston Road, London NW1 3BH

The publishers would like to thank the following
for allowing us to reproduce their pictures in
this book:
Alamy images: 20 (blickwinkel/fotototo). Corbis
images: 8 (Douglas Peebles), 18 (Eric Crichton).
Ecoscene: 14 (Sea Spring Photos). Garden Picture
Library: 6 (David Cavagnaro), 11 (Botanica), 22
(Friedrich Strauss). Getty images: title page and 9
(Wayne Eastep), 4 (Dan Kenyon), 10 (abiggerboat,
Inc), 12 (Ross M. Horowitz), 16 (Gabor Geissler),
17 (Olive Nichols), 19 (Marc O'Finley), 23 (Tobi
Corney). Photolibrary: cover and 15 (Botanica).
Wayland Picture Library: 5, 7, 13, 21.

Contents

What are vegetables?

Vegetables are the parts of a plant that we eat – the leaves, **roots, stems,** and **flowers**. Vegetable plants grow throughout the year. Different vegetables are ready to eat in different seasons.

Some vegetables, such as carrots, grow under the ground.

A **fruit** is the part of a plant that contains **seeds**. You might think that foods such as peppers, runner beans and courgettes are vegetables, but they are actually fruits.

▼ Can you guess which of these are vegetables and which are fruits?

Where do vegetables grow?

Look around your local area to see if you can spot vegetables growing. Some people have vegetable patches in their gardens where you might see asparagus, potatoes, spinach or rhubarb.

▼ People grow their own vegetables to eat at home.

Visit a market or supermarket and look at the vegetables on display – some may have been grown on farms nearby.

Vegetable Fact

Vegetables contain **vitamins and fibre**, which are important for us to eat to stay healthy.

The lettuces being planted on this farm will be sold in supermarkets.

Vegetables around the world

Vegetables are grown all over the world except near the freezing North and South Poles. Some vegetables such as yams, sweet potatoes and taro are important vegetable crops in **tropical** regions.

▼ These people are picking taro in Hawaii. People eat the taro's roots and leaves.

Others such as lettuce, watercress, cabbage and spinach grow well in countries where the temperature is cooler. Vegetables such as potatoes and onions grow in countries that have warm summers and colder winters.

These onions are being picked in Northern Europe.

Starting to grow

Some vegetables, such as onions, begin life as a **bulb**. Others, such as radishes, grow from seeds. Both seeds and bulbs contain food for the plant that will develop from them. When a seed begins to grow, it is called **germination**.

Roots grow down from the seed and a shoot grows upwards from it, pushing through the ground towards the light.

A shoot is growing from this onion bulb.

The roots of these radishes take in water and **nutrients** from the soil.

How plants make food

Leaves grow from the stem of a vegetable plant. The stem holds the leaves up to the light. The leaves use light, water and a gas called **carbon dioxide** from the air to make food for the plant.

▼ The leaves of plants contain **chlorophyll** which makes them green.

Vegetable plants such as potatoes and yams turn their food into a substance called **starch**, which fuels new growth.

▲ Eating starchy vegetables gives us **energy**.

Food from roots

Some of the vegetables we eat, such as carrots, beetroots, turnips, parsnips, radishes and swedes, are the roots of plants. The part of the plant we eat is the main root which grows larger than the other roots. This main root is called the **taproot**.

▼ These carrots are the main root of each carrot plant.

Vegetable Fact

Today's carrots are orange, but the world's first carrots were purple and yellow!

▼ Root vegetables like these beetroots have to be dug up from the ground.

Food from stems

Some of the vegetables we eat are the stems of plants. Some stem vegetables such as potatoes and yams grow under the ground. The ginger plant looks like a tall grass above ground, but the part we eat is the thick underground stem. Other stem vegetables such as rhubarb and celery grow above the ground.

Asparagus stems, sometimes called spears, have tiny leaves.

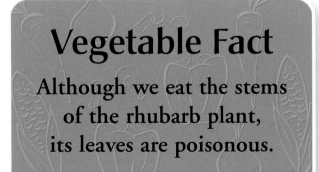

Vegetable Fact

Although we eat the stems of the rhubarb plant, its leaves are poisonous.

Ruby chard is a vegetable with red stems and green leaves.

Food from leaves and flowers

Some of the vegetables we eat are the leaves of plants. Most leaf vegetables such as watercress and spinach are green, but some types of spinach, cabbage and salad leaves are red or purple.

▼ Leaf vegetables grow in a variety of shapes, sizes and colours.

We eat the scented leaves of herb plants such as mint, parsley and coriander. Some vegetables such as cauliflower and broccoli are the plants' unopened flowers.

▲ We eat the flower buds of the globe artichoke.

How do we use vegetables?

We need to eat vitamin-rich vegetables to stay healthy. We eat some vegetables such as carrots, celery and spinach raw in salads. There are many ways of cooking vegetables – they can be boiled, fried, roasted and stewed.

▼ Vegetables are used to feed pets and farm animals.

Some vegetables such as onions and beetroot can be dried or pickled in vinegar. Medicines are made from vegetables, too.

▼ People all over the world eat vegetables to keep themselves healthy.

Grow your own vegetables

See how a vegetable plant grows for yourself. Try growing lettuces from seeds. Fill a seed tray with some compost. Plant some seeds by pushing them gently into the compost until they are well covered. Water the compost, then put the tray in a warm light place.

◀ Record what happens to your lettuce seeds.

▼ Plant the growing seedlings in your garden. Water them well.

Glossary

bulb
Some new plants grow from a bulb. The bulb contains food for the growing plant.

carbon dioxide
A gas in the air that plants use to make food.

chlorophyll
A substance in leaves that helps make a plant's food. It also makes leaves green.

energy
What we need to help us move, work and play.

fibre
A substance found in vegetables that is an important part of a good diet.

flowers
The parts of a flowering plant that have colourful, often scented, petals.

fruit
The part of a plant that contains seeds.

germination
The process by which a seeds starts to develop into a plant.

nutrients
Food in the soil that a plant needs for growth.

roots
The parts of a plant that keep it firmly in the ground and take in the water and nutrients it needs for growth.

seeds
Some new plants grow from a seed.

starch
The substance a plant produces to give it energy for growth.

stem
The part of a plant that holds it upright. We eat some swollen underground stems, such as potatoes and ginger.

taproot
The main root of a plant which swells into the root vegetables we eat.

tropical
Areas of the world where it is hot and wet.

vitamins
Substances found in fruits and vegetables that we eat to keep us healthy.

Index